READ WELL

Fantastic Frogs

Teacher's Guide

Read Well 1 • Unit 25

Ff

.

F says /fff/.
Continuous Sound
Quiet

Critical Foundations in Primary Reading

Marilyn Sprick, Lisa Howard, Ann Fidanque, Shelley V. Jones

Copyright 2007 (Second Edition) Sopris West Educational Services. All rights reserved.

ISBN 13-digit: 978-1-59318-448-3   ISBN 10-digit: 1-59318-448-4   131975/4-13

11 12 13 14 15 RRDHRBVA 17 16 15 14 13

Cambium
LEARNING®
Group

Voyager
LEARNING

Table of Contents
Unit 25
Fantastic Frogs

Read Well 1 Sequence and Sound Pronunciation Guide iv

Introduction 1
New and Important Objectives 2
Daily Lesson Planning 4
Materials and Materials Preparation 6

Important Tips

Multisyllabic Words 8
Acknowledging Accomplishments 9
Language and Vocabulary Practice—"Metamorphosis" and
High-Frequency Words 10

How to Teach the Lessons

Decoding Practice 1 12
Unit Introduction 14
Story 1, Duet 16
Skill Work Activity 1a 20
Comprehension Work Activity 1b 21
Story 2, Solo 22
Fact Summary 25
Comprehension Work Activity 2a 26
Skill Work Activity 2b 27

Decoding Practice 2 28
Story 3, Duet 30
Comprehension Work Activity 3 33

How to Teach the Lessons (*continued*)

Story 4, Solo 34
Comprehension Work Activity 4 37
Decoding Practice 3 38
Story 5, Duet 40
Story Summary 44
Comprehension Work Activity 5 45
Story 6, Solo 46
Comprehension Work Activity 6a 49
Skill Work Activity 6b 50

Decoding Practice 4 52

End of the Unit

Making Decisions 55
Unit 25 Oral Reading Fluency Assessment 56
Certificate of Achievement 57

Extra Practice 1 58
Extra Practice 1 Blackline Master 59
Extra Practice 1 Fluency Passage Blackline Master 60
Take-Home Game Blackline Master 61

Extra Practice 2 62
Extra Practice 2 Blackline Master 63
Extra Practice 2 Fluency Passages Blackline Master 64

Extra Practice 3 65
Extra Practice 3 Fluency Passage Blackline Master 66

Extra Practice 4 67
Extra Practice 4 Fluency Passage Blackline Master 68

I /I/ **I** Voiced (Word) **Unit A**	**Mm** /mmm/ **Monkey** Continuous Voiced **Unit B**	**Ss** /sss/ **Snake** Continuous Unvoiced **Unit 1**	**Ee** /eee/ **Emu** Continuous Voiced (Long) **Unit 2**	**ee** /eeee/ **Bee** Continuous Voiced (Long) **Unit 2**	**Mm** /mmm/ **Monkey** Continuous Voiced **Unit 3**
Aa /aaa/ **Ant** Continuous Voiced (Short) **Unit 4**	**Dd** /d/ **Dinosaur** Quick Voiced (not duh) **Unit 5**	**th** /ththth/ **the** Continuous Voiced **Unit 6**	**Nn** /nnn/ **Nest** Continuous Voiced **Unit 7**	**Tt** /t/ **Turkey** Quick Unvoiced (not tuh) **Unit 8**	**Ww** /www/ **Wind** Continuous Voiced (woo) **Unit 9**
Ii /iii/ **Insects** Continuous Voiced (Short) **Unit 10**	**Th** /Ththth/ **The** Continuous Voiced **Unit 10**	**Hh** /h/ **Hippo** Quick Unvoiced (not huh) **Unit 11**	**Cc** /c/ **Cat** Quick Unvoiced (not cuh) **Unit 12**	**Rr** /rrr/ **Rabbit** Continuous Voiced **Unit 13**	**ea** /eaeaea/ **Eagle** Continuous Voiced (Long) **Unit 13**
Sh/sh /shshsh/ **Sheep** Continuous Unvoiced **Unit 14**	**Kk, -ck** /k/ **Kangaroo** Quick Unvoiced (not kuh) **Unit 15**	**oo** /oooo/ **Moon** Continuous Voiced (Long) **Unit 16**	**ar** /ar/ **Shark** Voiced (R-Controlled) **Unit 17**	**Wh/wh** /wh/ **Whale** Quick Voiced **Unit 18**	**Ee** /ĕĕĕ/ **Engine or Ed** Continuous Voiced (Short) **Unit 19**
-y /-yyy/ **Fly** Continuous Voiced (Long) **Unit 20**	**Ll** /lll/ **Letter** Continuous Voiced **Unit 21**	**Oo** /ooo/ **Otter** Continuous Voiced (Short) **Unit 22**	**Bb** /b/ **Bat** Quick Voiced (not buh) **Unit 23**	**all** /all/ **Ball** Voiced **Unit 23**	**Gg** /g/ **Gorilla** Quick Voiced (not guh) **Unit 24**
Ff /fff/ **Frog** Continuous Unvoiced **Unit 25**	**Uu** /uuu/ **Umbrella** Continuous Voiced (Short) **Unit 26**	**er** /er/ **Sister** Voiced (R-Controlled) **Unit 27**	**oo** /oo/ **Book** Voiced (Short) **Unit 27**	**Yy** /y-/ **Yarn** Quick Voiced **Unit 28**	**Aa** /a/ **Ago** Voiced (Schwa) **Unit 28**
Pp /p/ **Pig** Quick Unvoiced (not puh) **Unit 29**	**ay** /ay/ **Hay** Voiced **Unit 29**	**Vv** /vvv/ **Volcano** Continuous Voiced **Unit 30**	**Qu/qu** /qu/ **Quake** Quick Unvoiced **Unit 31**	**Jj** /j/ **Jaguar** Quick Voiced (not juh) **Unit 32**	**Xx** /ksss/ **Fox** Continuous Unvoiced **Unit 33**
or /or/ **Horn** Voiced (R-Controlled) **Unit 33**	**Zz** /zzz/ **Zebra** Continuous Voiced **Unit 34**	**a_e** /a_e/ **Cake** Bossy E Voiced (Long) **Unit 34**	**-y** /-y/ **Baby** Voiced **Unit 35**	**i_e** /i_e/ **Kite** Bossy E Voiced (Long) **Unit 35**	**ou** /ou/ **Cloud** Voiced **Unit 36**
ow /ow/ **Cow** Voiced **Unit 36**	**Ch/ch** /ch/ **Chicken** Quick Unvoiced **Unit 37**	**ai** /ai/ **Rain** Voiced (Long) **Unit 37**	**igh** /igh/ **Flight** Voiced (Long) **Unit 38**	**o_e** /o_e/ **Bone** Bossy E Voiced (Long) **Unit 38**	**ir** /ir/ **Bird** Voiced (R-Controlled) **Unit 38**

Introduction
Fantastic Frogs

Story Notes

This unit builds upon the content knowledge of previous units. Children learn more about metamorphosis by tracing the life cycle of a frog. They also make connections with prior knowledge—learning that tadpoles, like sharks, breathe through gills. Next, children read a fictional story about a frog who briefly enjoys good meals while in captivity. Finally, children read a poem about three frogs on a log.

Recommended Read Aloud

For reading outside of small group instruction

From Tadpole to Frog by Wendy Pfeffer

Factual, Information-Based

Follow the life cycle of frogs through the seasons of the year. Vivid pictures help children learn about each stage of metamorphosis and development. View thousands of eggs hatching into tadpoles. Learn how tadpoles hide from their predators and hibernate through the cold winter. Follow these interesting animals as they finally transition from tadpoles into adult frogs.

Read Well Connection

In the *Read Well* stories, a frog named Fred helps introduce the life cycle of a frog. Information in *From Tadpole to Frog* both reinforces and expands children's understanding of this metamorphosis.

NOTE FROM THE AUTHORS

**LEAPING FORWARD
(Reminder)**

If your students exceeded the fluency goals on the Unit 24 Assessment, we encourage you to skip Unit 25.

Because the stories in this unit are favorites of staff and students, you may wish to have children read the stories at home.

New and Important Objectives
A Research-Based Reading Program
Just Right for Young Children

Oral Language
Phonemic Awareness
Phonics
Fluency
Vocabulary
Comprehension

◆◆ Oral Language

In Units 21–38, language patterns are provided for high-frequency words and for some of the low-frequency words that are likely to require clarification. For English Language Learners and children with language delays, see page 10 for a list of the new high-frequency patterns.

Phonemic Awareness

Isolating Beginning, Middle, Ending Sounds, Segmenting, Blending, Rhyming, Onset and Rime

Phonics

Letter Sounds, Combinations, and Affixes
★ *Ff*
★ *fr-*, ★ *fl-*, ★ *-ing*
Review • *Ss, Ee, ee, Mm, Aa, Dd, th, Nn, Tt, Ww, Ii, Th, Hh, Cc, Rr, ea, sh, Sh, Kk, -ck, oo, ar, wh, Wh, e (short), -y (as in "fly"), Ll, Oo, Bb, all, Gg*

F says /fff/.
Funny flying frog,
/F/, /f/, /fff/.

Continuous Sound

Pattern Words
★ *call,* ★ *dog,* ★ *facts,* ★ *Facts,* ★ *fall,* ★ *fantastic,* ★ *Fantastic,* ★ *fast,* ★ *fat,* ★ *feed,* ★ *feet,* ★ *fell,* ★ *fifteen,* ★ *fill,* ★ *fin,* ★ *finish,* ★ *fins,* ★ *fish,* ★ *Fish,* ★ *fit,* ★ *fly,* ★ *Fly,* ★ *food,* ★ *Fran,* ★ *Fran's,* ★ *Fred,* ★ *Fred's,* ★ *free,* ★ *frog,* ★ *Frog,* ★ *Frogs,* ★ *fry,* ★ *gill,* ★ *gills,* ★ *hog,* ★ *If,* ★ *insect,* ★ *insects,* ★ *log,* ★ *Log,* ★ *marsh,* ★ *meal,* ★ *nearby,* ★ *rang,* ★ *ring,* ★ *sang,* ★ *sitting,* ★ *softball,* ★ *song,* ★ *thinking,* ★ *wings*

Review • *all, am, an, and, at, At, back, bad, ball, be, began, best, big, Big, Bill, blast, bog, bring, by, can, cannot, can't, car, cool, clean, dad, Dad, did, didn't, dress, eat, eats, get, got, green, had, hard, he, He, Hear, hid, in, In, it, It, It's, kick, Kim, land, last, let, little, long, lot, me, mom, my, My, need, needed, net, Nick, nodded, not, Not, on, ran, sat, see, See, She, sing, small, smart, Soon, stick, still, strong, swam, swim, swoosh, tall, tank, Tank, thank, that, That, Then, thing, think, this, This, three, Three, too, tree, trick, Trish, we, weeds, well, Well, wet, wheel, When, will, wing, With*

◆◆ = Oral language patterns   ★ = New in this unit

2

Phonics *(continued)*

Tricky Words

⭐ *egg*, ⭐ *eggs*, ⭐ *legs*, ⭐ *work*

Review • *a, A, about, are, because, go, has, his, His, I, is, isn't, listen, Listen, Look, no, No, one, said, should, so, So, the, The, there, There, to, two, want, wanted, was, what, What, where, Where, Who, would*

Comprehension

Comprehension Strategies

Building Knowledge, Priming Background Knowledge, Making Connections, Predicting, Identifying, Describing, Defining, Explaining, Inferring, Affirming, Responding, Visualizing, Questioning, Summarizing, Sequencing

Story Elements

Title, Where (Setting), Who (Main Character), Problem, What (Action)

Story Vocabulary

⭐ Tadpole

Text Structure

Beginning, Middle, End

Expository Elements

Fact

Genre

Nonfiction • Expository

Fiction • Narrative With Factual Content

Poem

Lessons

Each animal has its own way of adapting to its environment. (First introduced in Unit 13)

⭐ Facts can help you identify and classify animals.

Written Response

Sentence Completion, Sentence Writing, Sentence Comprehension—Multiple Choice, Summarizing—Story Map, Conventions—Periods, Capitals (Beginning of a Sentence)

Fluency

Accuracy, Expression, Phrasing, Rate

Daily Lesson Planning

PACING

Some students will begin the process of learning to read slowly but make rapid progress later. To be at grade level by the end of the year, most first graders need to complete Unit 30 by the end of the 27th week of school. Groups that are working at a slower pace may require more intensive *Read Well* instruction and practice. (See *Getting Started: A Guide to Implementation.*)

ASSESSMENT

Upon completion of this unit, assess each student and proceed to Unit 26 as appropriate.

SAMPLE LESSON PLANS

The sample lesson plans illustrate how materials can be used for students with different learning needs. Each lesson plan is designed to provide daily decoding practice and story reading.

2-DAY PLAN • *Acceleration*

Day 1	Day 2
• Decoding Practice 1	• Decoding Practice 2
• Stories 1 and 2 and Fact Summary	• Stories 3 and 5 and Story Summary
• Comprehension Work 1b*	• Comprehension Work 3*
• Comprehension Work 2a*	• Comprehension Work 5*
• Homework 1, Story 2*	• Homework 2, Story 4*
	• Homework 3, Story 6*

In this 2-Day Plan, students skip Decoding Practice 3 and 4 and Stories 4 and 6. (Stories 4 and 6 are included in the homework schedule.) Do not assign Comprehension Work 4 and 6a unless students have read the stories.

3-DAY PLAN

Day 1	Day 2	Day 3
• Decoding Practice 1	• Decoding Practice 2	• Decoding Practice 3
• Stories 1 and 2 and Fact Summary	• Stories 3 and 4	• Story 5, Story Summary, and Story 6
• Comprehension Work 1b*	• Comprehension Work 3*	• Comprehension Work 5*
• Comprehension Work 2a*	• Comprehension Work 4*	• Comprehension Work 6a*
• Homework 1, Story 2*	• Homework 2, Story 4*	• Homework 3, Story 6*
		• Homework 4, Storybook Decoding Review*

To avoid excessive seatwork, 2-, 3-, and 4-Day Plans omit or adjust use of Skill Work. If appropriate, Skill Work 1a, 2b, and 6b can be used anytime during or after this unit as independent work or homework.

4-DAY PLAN

Day 1	Day 2	Day 3	Day 4
• Decoding Practice 1	• Decoding Practice 2	• Decoding Practice 3	• Decoding Practice 4
• Stories 1 and 2 and Fact Summary	• Stories 3 and 4	• Story 5, Story Summary, and Story 6	• Review Stories 2, 4, and 6
• Comprehension Work 1b*	• Comprehension Work 3*	• Comprehension Work 5*	• Comprehension Work 6a*
• Comprehension Work 2a*	• Comprehension Work 4*	• Homework 3, Story 6*	• Homework 4, Storybook Decoding Review*
• Homework 1, Story 2*	• Homework 2, Story 4*		

* From *Read Well* Comprehension and Skill Work (workbook), *Read Well* Homework (blackline masters), or Extra Practice in this book.

6-DAY PLAN • *Pre-Intervention*

Day 1	Day 2	Day 3
• Decoding Practice 1 • Story 1 • Skill Work 1a* (Optional) • Comprehension Work 1b*	• Review Decoding Practice 1 • Story 2 and Fact Summary • Comprehension Work 2a* • Skill Work 2b* (Optional) • Homework 1, Story 2*	• Decoding Practice 2 • Story 3 • Comprehension Work 3*
Day 4	**Day 5**	**Day 6**
• Review Decoding Practice 2 • Story 4 • Comprehension Work 4* • Homework 2, Story 4*	• Decoding Practice 3 • Story 5 and Story Summary • Comprehension Work 5* • Homework 4, Storybook Decoding Review*	• Decoding Practice 4 • Story 6 • Comprehension Work 6a* • Skill Work 6b* (Optional) • Homework 3, Story 6*

PRE-INTERVENTION AND INTERVENTION

See *Getting Started: A Guide to Implementation* for information on how to achieve mastery at a faster pace with students who require six or more days of instruction.

8-DAY PLAN • *Intervention*

Day 1	Day 2	Day 3	Day 4
• Decoding Practice 1 • Story 1 • Skill Work 1a* (Optional) • Comprehension Work 1b*	• Review Decoding Practice 1 • Story 2 and Fact Summary • Comprehension Work 2a* • Skill Work 2b* (Optional) • Homework 1, Story 2*	• Decoding Practice 2 • Story 3 • Comprehension Work 3*	• Review Decoding Practice 2 • Story 4 • Comprehension Work 4* • Homework 2, Story 4*
Day 5	**Day 6**	**Day 7**	**Day 8**
• Decoding Practice 3 • Story 5 and Story Summary • Comprehension Work 5* • Homework 4, Storybook Decoding Review*	• Decoding Practice 4 • Story 6 • Comprehension Work 6a* • Skill Work 6b* (Optional) • Homework 3, Story 6*	• Extra Practice 1* • Extra Practice 1 Fluency Passage*	• Extra Practice 2* • Extra Practice 2 Fluency Passages*

10-DAY PLAN • *Intervention*

Day 1	Day 2	Day 3	Day 4	Day 5
• Decoding Practice 1 • Story 1 • Skill Work 1a* (Optional) • Comprehension Work 1b*	• Review Decoding Practice 1 • Story 2 and Fact Summary • Comprehension Work 2a* • Skill Work 2b* (Optional) • Homework 1, Story 2*	• Decoding Practice 2 • Story 3 • Comprehension Work 3*	• Review Decoding Practice 2 • Story 4 • Comprehension Work 4* • Homework 2, Story 4*	• Decoding Practice 3 • Story 5 and Story Summary • Comprehension Work 5* • Homework 4, Storybook Decoding Review*
Day 6	**Day 7**	**Day 8**	**Day 9**	**Day 10**
• Decoding Practice 4 • Story 6 • Comprehension Work 6a* • Skill Work 6b* (Optional) • Homework 3, Story 6*	• Extra Practice 1* • Extra Practice 1 Fluency Passage*	• Extra Practice 2* • Extra Practice 2 Fluency Passages*	• Extra Practice 3* • Extra Practice 3 Fluency Passage*	• Extra Practice 4* • Extra Practice 4 Fluency Passage*

Materials and Materials Preparation

 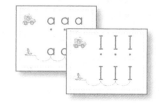  

Core Lessons

Teacher Materials

READ WELL MATERIALS

- Unit 25 Teacher's Guide
- Sound and Word Cards for Units 1–25
- Game markers (optional for use with cover-up activities)
- *Assessment Manual* or page 56

SCHOOL SUPPLIES

- Stopwatch or watch with a second hand

Student Materials

READ WELL MATERIALS

- Decoding Book 3 for each student
- Unit 25 Storybook for each student
- Unit 25 Comprehension and Skill Work for each student (My Activity Book 3)
- Unit 25 Certificate of Achievement (blackline master page 57)
- Unit 25 Homework for each student (blackline masters)
  See *Getting Started* for suggested homework routines.

SCHOOL SUPPLIES

- Pencils, colors (optional—markers, crayons, or colored pencils)

Make one copy per student of each blackline master as appropriate for the group.

Note: For new or difficult Comprehension and Skill Work activities, make overhead transparencies from the blackline masters. Use the transparencies to demonstrate and guide practice.

Extra Practice Lessons

Note: Use these lessons only if needed.

Student Materials

READ WELL MATERIALS

- Unit 25 Extra Practice 1 and 2 for each student (blackline master pages 59 and 63)
- Unit 25 Extra Practice 1, 2, 3, and 4 Fluency Passages for each student (blackline master pages 60, 64, 66, and 68)

SCHOOL SUPPLIES

- Pencils, colors (markers, crayons, or colored pencils)
- White boards or paper

Important Tips

In this section, you will find:

Multisyllabic Words

Teaching children how to read words doesn't stop with single-syllable words. To be independent readers, children need to know how to apply their skills to multisyllabic words.

CELEBRATE EVERY ACCOMPLISHMENT, BIG OR SMALL!

Acknowledging Accomplishments

Your enthusiasm will motivate even those who struggle. This tip will help you learn how other teachers cheer their students on.

Language and Vocabulary Practice— "Metamorphosis" and High-Frequency Words

An additional focus on vocabulary and language skills often benefits English Language Learners and students with language delays.

Preview and review the vocabulary word "metamorphosis" before story reading. Recursive use of the word "metamorphosis" provides students with an opportunity to deepen their conceptual knowledge of the word.

A list of oral language patterns used with high-frequency words is also provided for additional emphasis and practice across settings.

Multisyllabic Words

In addition to mastering beginning reading skills, children need to learn how to apply skills to multisyllabic words.

INITIAL STRATEGIES

From Unit 16, *Read Well* has gradually incorporated instruction and practice of multisyllabic words—first using the words in listening and speaking, and then introducing the words in decoding practice and story reading.

For example, in the first Duet Story in Unit 16, students first develop knowledge of the word "raccoon" within the context of the Duet Story. Students develop the oral (speaking) vocabulary through identification of "raccoon" as a rebus word and through aural (listening) knowledge of the word "raccoon." Next, the written word "raccoon" is introduced within an exercise that has students identify the known word parts and then put them together. Visually the words are introduced within a familiar equation.

rac • coon = raccoon

Read the first word part. (rac)
Next word part. (coon)
Read the big word. (raccoon)

In Unit 24, students are introduced to the slightly irregular, multisyllabic word "gorilla." The word is rehearsed through listening and speaking with the Alphabet Poem, "<u>G</u> as in Gorilla." Then the word is introduced within a Tricky Word exercise.

Gorilla

This new word begins with /g/. It's a little tricky, but try to figure it out. Sound it out in your head, then keep it a secret until I count to five.

As they move forward, *Read Well* students learn to identify mutlisyllabic words with word family practice ("little," "settle," "rattle," "doodle," and "needle"), and with the familiar Accuracy and Fluency procedure—reading the underlined part of a word and then the whole word (e.g., "<u>need</u>ed," "<u>want</u>ed").

BUILDING SELF-CONFIDENCE

Watch for the Multisyllabic Challenge Words in Decoding Practice 4 (e.g., "telegram," "basketball," "fantastic"). Young children begin seeing themselves as readers when they can read big words all by themselves!

Acknowledging Accomplishments

PURPOSE

Some children are internally motivated to learn new skills. Other children need your guidance and support. Use words, gadgets, and gimmicks to keep the children excited about their accomplishments.

TEACH WITH ENTHUSIASM!
(Reminder)
All children are motivated by your acknowledgement of their efforts and accomplishments.

When students meet your expectations, acknowledge individuals and provide descriptive feedback.

• [Kaitlin], you kept your place.
• [Misha], you waited for your turn.
• [Tom], your finger was in the right place.

Provide attention with privileges.

• [Naomi], you kept your place, so you get the next turn.
• [Jacob], you waited for your turn, so you get to help me be the teacher. Tell the group which row to read.

Be silly.

• Each time I hear you read the hard word, I'll quack like a duck.

Use physical demonstrations.

• [Nick], let me shake your hand. You read the hard word "could."
• [Everyone], pat yourself on the back.
• [Everyone], air clap for [Sally]. She read each word carefully.
• [Ahmed], show me a big smile.
• [Lakeesha], give me five!
• You worked hard on the Tricky Words. I'm going to erase each word that you can read without my help.

Use gimmicks and gadgets.

• [Hector], your finger is in the right place, so you get to use the pointer.
• [Sally] waited for her turn, so she gets to use the spring toy.

Use sticky notes and notes home that congratulate students and encourage them to practice.

• [Jake], you can read the Tricky Words, so I'm going to write them on a sticky note. You earned the words "could," "would," and "should."

When all students have passed a unit, present the Certificates of Achievement with a small celebration.

Language and Vocabulary Practice "Metamorphosis" and High-Frequency Words

PURPOSE

The following review and practice strategy may be used to augment a structured oral language program.

PREVIEW "METAMORPHOSIS" BEFORE READING UNIT 25

In Unit 25, students revisit the concept of metamorphosis—applying their prior knowledge of the metamorphosis of a butterfly to that of a frog.

- Collect pictures of insects and other animals going through a metamorphosis.

- Using the pictures, say something like:

  Your vocabulary word is "metamorphosis." Tell me the word. (Metamorphosis)

  A *metamorphosis* is a change that some animals go through as they grow up.

  Show students a picture of the metamorphosis of a butterfly.

  We read about a metamorphosis a long time ago.

  Point to the egg. We read about an insect that begins as an . . . (egg).

  Point to the caterpillar. The egg changes into a . . . (caterpillar).

  The caterpillar develops into a . . . (chrysalis)

  and finally becomes a . . . (butterfly).

  What are all those changes called? (A metamorphosis)

  Repeat with other pictures.

- Have students define the word "metamorphosis." Say something like:

  A change that some animals go through as they grow up is called a . . . metamorphosis.

  What is a metamorphosis? (A change that some animals go through as they grow up)

◆◆ **FOR ENGLISH LANGUAGE LEARNERS AND CHILDREN WITH LANGUAGE DELAYS**

REVIEW "METAMORPHOSIS" AFTER READING UNIT 25

Review the vocabulary word after the story. Use pictures or have children draw pictures of a metamorphosis.

ORAL LANGUAGE PATTERNS USED WITH NEW HIGH-FREQUENCY WORDS

Sentences from *Read Well* Decoding Practice are repeated below for additional language practice.

ORAL LANGUAGE PATTERNS ⭐ High-Frequency Words Introduced in This Unit
⭐ A [jet] moves *fast.* How does a [jet] move? (A [jet] moves *fast.*)
⭐ Fred was a big, *fat* frog? What kind of frog was Fred? (A big, *fat* frog)
⭐ A *fly* is an insect. What is an insect? (A *fly*)
⭐ Insects are *food* for a frog. What are insects? (*Food* for a frog)
⭐ A [frog eats] *if* [he is hungry]. When does [he eat]? (*If* [he is hungry])
⭐ Fred loves to *sing.* What does Fred love to do? (Fred loves to *sing.*)
⭐ We *work* hard. What do we do? (We *work* hard.)

How to Teach the Lessons

Teach from this section. Each instructional component is outlined in an easy-to-teach format. Special tips are provided to help you nurture student progress.

Decoding Practice 1

- Unit Introduction
- Story 1, Duet
- Skill Work Activity 1a
- Comprehension Work Activity 1b
- Story 2, Solo
- Fact Summary
- Comprehension Work Activity 2a
- Skill Work Activity 2b

Decoding Practice 2

- Story 3, Duet
- Comprehension Work Activity 3
- Story 4, Solo
- Comprehension Work Activity 4

Decoding Practice 3

- Story 5, Duet
- Story Summary
- Comprehension Work Activity 5
- Story 6, Solo
- Comprehension Work Activity 6a
- Skill Work Activity 6b

Decoding Practice 4

Review Solo Stories

> **BUILDING INDEPENDENCE**
> **Next Steps • Principles of Instruction**
>
> For Units 21–38, follow the scaffolded principles of instruction below.
>
> Provide demonstration and/or guided practice only with:
> - New sounds
> - Pattern words with new sounds
> - New Tricky Words
> - New multisyllabic words
>
> Provide independent practice (practice without your assistance or voice) on:
> - New and review pattern words with known sounds
> - Review Tricky Words
> - Review multisyllabic words
>
> If students make errors, provide appropriate corrections.
> - Have students identify any difficult sound and then sound out the word. Provide discrimination practice.
> - Reintroduce difficult Tricky Words based on the initial introduction procedures.
>
> If students require your assistance on words with known sounds, evaluate placement and consider a Jell-Well Review.

① SOUND REVIEW

② NEW SOUND INTRODUCTION

③ NEW SOUND PRACTICE

◆◆ **④** SOUNDING OUT SMOOTHLY
★ **New blends: /Fr-/ and /fl-/**
"Fred" and "fly" represent the first times students read the /Fr-/ and /fl-/ blends. Demonstrate and guide practice as needed.

★ **Multiple meanings: "fly"**
Note: Students practice using the word "fly" as a verb and a noun in oral sentences.
- For each word, have students say the underlined part, sound out the word, and then read the word.
  Use the words in sentences as needed.
- Provide repeated practice. Mix group and individual turns, independent of your voice.

Note: If the /-ct/ blend in "facts" is difficult, have students sound out "act" first, then "fact," and finally "facts." Have them use "fact" and "facts" in sentences.
(I know one *fact* about insects. You know many *facts* about insects.)

⑤ MULTISYLLABIC WORDS
★ **New affix: /-ing/**
- For each word, have students first *say* each of the word's parts and then read the whole word.
  Say something like:
  Read the first word part. (be)
  Next word part. (gan)
  Read the big word. (began)
  If students have difficulty, have them *sound out* each of the word parts, then read each part, and then read the whole word.
- Repeat, mixing group and individual turns, independent of your voice. Use the words in sentences as needed.

⑥ TRICKY WORDS
★ **New Tricky Words: "eggs" and "legs"**
The words "eggs" and "legs" are pronounced differently by different people. Tell students that the words are a little tricky. Have them sound out the words and then say the words they hear. Have the students use "eggs" and "legs" in sentences.
- Have students read the row.
- Repeat, mixing group and individual turns, independent of your voice.

⑦ DAILY STORY READING
Proceed to the Unit 25 Storybook. See Daily Lesson Planning for pacing suggestions.

⑧ COMPREHENSION AND SKILL WORK ACTIVITY 1 AND/OR ACTIVITY 2
See pages 20, 21 and/or 26, 27.

Note: The light scripting in *Read Well* will help you visualize instruction as you prepare for a lesson. Scripting provides an instructional guide and is not intended to be memorized or read to students.

UNIT **25** DECODING PRACTICE I
(For use with Stories 1 and 2)

1. SOUND REVIEW Use Sound Cards for Units 1–24.

2. NEW SOUND INTRODUCTION Have students echo (repeat) the phrases. Do not have students read the poem.

F̲ as in F̲rog
Capital letter F̲, small letter f̲,
F̲ says fff.
F̲unny f̲lying f̲rog,
F, f, fff.

★3. NEW SOUND PRACTICE Have students read, trace, and say /fff/. Next, have students trace and sound out "Frog," then read the word "Frog."

F	f	F̲rog

★4. SOUNDING OUT SMOOTHLY For each word, have students say any underlined part, sound out the word in one smooth breath, and then read the word.

▲

★F̲red   ★f̲ly   F̲acts   f̲ish

✿ last   get   gills   wing

★5. MULTISYLLABIC WORDS Have students say each word part, then read the whole word.

● be·gan = began   ★think·ing = thinking

☆fan·tas·tic = fantastic   in·sect = insect

★6. TRICKY WORDS Introduce "eggs" and "legs" using the Tricky Word procedure. Have students silently figure out each word and then read it aloud.

✈ ★eggs   ★legs   because   about

7. DAILY STORY READING

5

Sentence Suggestions: If a sentence is included, use it *after* decoding the individual word. The sentences may be used to build oral language patterns and vocabulary. Use of sentences also emphasizes that words have meaning.

① **INTRODUCING THE UNIT AND THE TITLE PAGE**

Identifying—Title

Tell students this unit is called "Fantastic Frogs."

Predicting

Ask students what they think they already know about frogs.

② **INTRODUCING VOCABULARY**

Vocabulary—Tadpole, Gills, Insect, Metamorphosis

Tadpole

Put your finger under the first picture.

A *tadpole* is an animal that lives in the water. It grows into a frog or a toad.

Gills

Put your finger under the next picture.

Gills are what fish use to breathe oxygen from the water. Sharks have . . . (gills).

Insect

Put your finger under the next picture.

An *insect* is an animal that has six legs and three body parts. Name some insects you know.

Metamorphosis

Put your finger under the next picture.

A *metamorphosis* is a change. A caterpillar goes through a metamorphosis to become a butterfly. What else do you think goes through a metamorphosis?

Fantastic Frogs

Illustrated by Ursula Vernon

Fantastic Frog Facts
By Marilyn Sprick

Fred's Fish Tank
By Marilyn Sprick and Shelley V. Jones

Three Frogs on a Log
By Shelley V. Jones

UNIT 25 STORIES

Fantastic Frog Facts
Chapter 1, Metamorphosis 24
Chapter 2, Fred's Frog Facts 27
Fact Summary... 29

Fred's Fish Tank
Chapter 1, Captured 30
Chapter 2, In the Tank 32
Chapter 3, A Night With Fred......................... 34
Story Summary 37

Three Frogs on a Log 38
Storybook Decoding Review 40

Vocabulary Words

tadpole	gills	insect	metamorphosis
A tadpole is an animal that lives in the water. It grows into a frog or a toad.	Gills are what fish use to breathe oxygen from the water.	An insect is an animal that has six legs and three body parts.	A metamorphosis is a change. A caterpillar goes through a metamorphosis to become a butterfly.

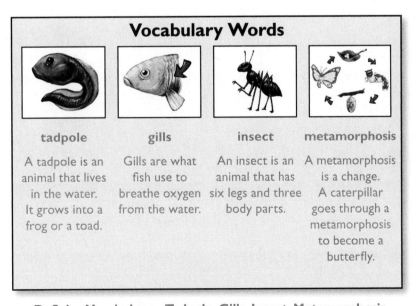

Vocabulary Words

tadpole	gills	insect	metamorphosis
A tadpole is an animal that lives in the water. It grows into a frog or a toad.	Gills are what fish use to breathe oxygen from the water.	An insect is an animal that has six legs and three body parts.	A metamorphosis is a change. A caterpillar goes through a metamorphosis to become a butterfly.

Defining Vocabulary—Tadpole, Gills, Insect, Metamorphosis

DUET STORY READING INSTRUCTIONS
Students read from their own storybooks.
The teacher reads the small text and students read the large text.

PACING
- 2- to 4-Day Plans: Have students do the first reading
  of Duet Story 1.
  Then proceed to repeated readings of Solo Story 2.
- 6- to 10-Day Plans: Have students do the first *and*
  second readings as needed.

COMPREHENSION BUILDING:
DISCUSSION QUESTIONS AND TEACHER THINK ALOUDS
- Ask questions and discuss text on the first reading when indicated in
  the storybook in light gray text.
- Encourage students to answer questions with complete sentences
  when appropriate. Following a response, acknowledge the accuracy
  of the response and then say something like:
  That's right. Fred is looking for a tadpole. Start your answer with "Fred is."
  (Fred is looking for a tadpole.)
- If students have difficulty with a comprehension question, think aloud
  with them or reread the portion of the story that answers the question.
  Then, ask the question again.

PROCEDURES
1. First Reading
Mix group and individual turns on student-read sentences. On individual
turns, gently correct any error, and then have the student reread the text.

2. Second Reading
Repeat the reading only as needed for comprehension.

Note: Questions focus students on important story elements and provide prompts
for story discussions. Answers provide guidance, not verbatim responses.

STORY 1, DUET

Fantastic Frog Facts

CHAPTER 1

Metamorphosis

In an earlier unit, we learned that a caterpillar becomes a butterfly. This change is called a metamorphosis.

In this story, Fred the frog learns that frogs go through a metamorphosis. Look at the picture.

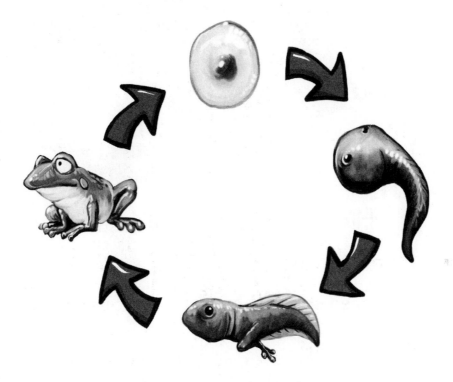

First there is an egg. A tadpole hatches from an egg. Then the tadpole grows legs. Finally, the tadpole changes into a frog. Touch the frog.

Let's trace the metamorphosis a frog goes through.¹ First there's an egg. Touch under the egg. What happens to the egg?² Touch under the tadpole. What happens to the tadpole?³ Touch under the tadpole with legs. What does the tadpole become when it is an adult?⁴ What are these changes called?⁵

24

❶ **Using Vocabulary—Metamorphosis**

❷ **Explaining** (The egg changes into a tadpole.)

❸ **Explaining** (It grows legs.)

❹ **Explaining** (A tadpole becomes a frog.)

❺ **Using Vocabulary—Metamorphosis** (The changes are called a metamorphosis.)

Fred said, "I see a fish."

FINGER TRACKING
(Reminder)
Continue having children track the large text with their fingers.

His mom said, "That isn't a fish. It's a little frog."

Fred said, "It can't be, because a frog has legs."

Fred's mom said, "When a frog is small it has no legs."

"What?" said Fred.

What is Fred looking at? |

25

❶ **Identifying—What** (Fred is looking at a tadpole.)

STORY I, DUET

Fred's mom smiled. She said, "First you were an egg, then a tadpole. That little animal that looks like a fish is called a tadpole. You grew legs and became a frog. See the little legs on the tadpoles."

Fred looked closely.

What is happening to the tadpoles?[1]

Fred thought for a while. Then he said, "Frogs breathe air. If I was a tadpole, how did I breathe?"

"A fish has gills," said Fred's mom.

"A little frog has gills too."

Touch the tadpole's gills.[2] What does the tadpole use its gills for?[3]

Fred began to think hard. At last

he said, "I think I get it.

First I was an egg. Next I was a tadpole. Then I grew legs and became a big green frog!"

Fred's mom said,

"What a smart frog!"

Let's describe the metamorphosis a frog goes through. What happens first?[4]

26

❶ **Explaining** (The tadpoles are growing legs.)

❷ **Identifying—Where, Using Vocabulary—Gills**

❸ **Making Connections, Inferring, Using Vocabulary—Gills** (The tadpole uses its gills to breathe.)

❹ **Explaining, Defining Vocabulary—Metamorphosis** (The egg becomes a tadpole. The tadpole grows legs. The tadpole changes into a frog.)

SOUND PAGE

Use work pages from the workbook.

UNIT 25 SKILL WORK ACTIVITY 1a   Name _____ ▲
SOUND PAGE: For use after Story 1

© Sopris West Educational Services. All rights reserved.   11

PROCEDURES

For each step, demonstrate and guide practice as needed.

1. Handwriting—Basic Instructions

- Have students identify the capital letter F̲.
- Have students trace and write the capital letter F̲—leaving a finger space between each letter. Repeat with the small letter f̲ on the second two rows.
- In each row have students circle their best letter.

2. Drawing Pictures That Begin With /fff/—Basic Instructions

- Have students fill the box with things that begin with /fff/. Students can write the letter f̲, draw pictures of things that begin with /fff/, cut out and paste on pictures of things that begin with /fff/, or cut out and paste on words that begin with /fff/.

Note: Neat work helps students take pride in their efforts.

FACT SHEET

Use work pages from the workbook.

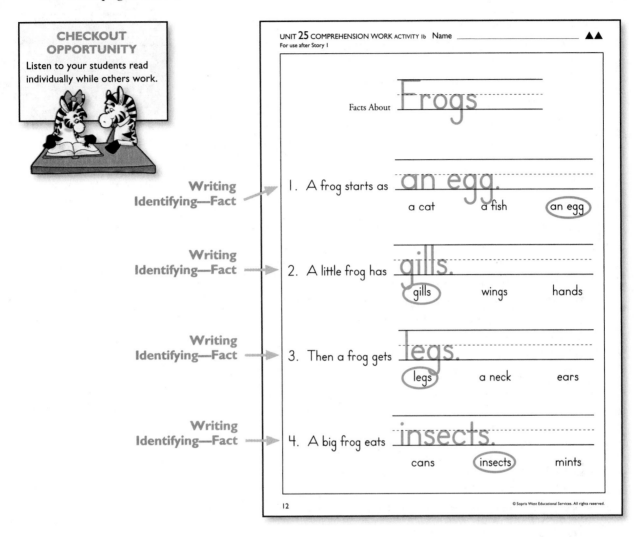

CHECKOUT OPPORTUNITY

Listen to your students read individually while others work.

UNIT **25** COMPREHENSION WORK ACTIVITY Ib   Name _____   ▲▲
For use after Story 1

Facts About ___Frogs___

Writing Identifying—Fact
1. A frog starts as ___an egg.___
   a cat   a fish   (an egg)

Writing Identifying—Fact
2. A little frog has ___gills.___
   (gills)   wings   hands

Writing Identifying—Fact
3. Then a frog gets ___legs.___
   (legs)   a neck   ears

Writing Identifying—Fact
4. A big frog eats ___insects.___
   cans   (insects)   mints

12

PROCEDURES

For each step, demonstrate and guide practice as needed.

- (Demonstrate) Have students orally respond to items while you demonstrate how to complete the page.
- (Guide) Have students orally respond to the items, but do not demonstrate how to complete the page.
- (Independent With Support) Have students silently read over the items and ask any questions they may have.

Multiple Choice, Sentence Completion—Basic Instructions

- Have students select and circle the word or words that correctly complete the sentences. Periodically, think aloud with students. Discuss the multiple choice options. As appropriate, ask questions like: "Does the first answer make sense?" "Is that what the book said?" "Is the answer completely correct?"
- Have them write answers in the blanks and place a period at the end.

SOLO STORY READING INSTRUCTIONS

Students read from their own storybooks.

COMPREHENSION BUILDING:
DISCUSSION QUESTIONS AND TEACHER THINK ALOUDS

- Ask questions and discuss text on the first reading when indicated in the storybook in light gray text.
- Encourage students to answer questions with complete sentences when appropriate.
- If students have difficulty with a comprehension question, think aloud with them or reread the portion of the story that answers the question. Then, ask the question again.

PROCEDURES

1. First Reading

- Mix group and individual turns on student-read sentences. On individual turns, gently correct any error, and then have the student reread the text.
- After students complete the first reading and before the second reading, have students practice a paragraph. First demonstrate expressive reading for students, then give individual turns. Acknowledge student efforts.

2. Second Reading

- Mix group and individual turns, independent of your voice.
  Have students work toward an accuracy goal of 0–2 errors.
  Quietly keep track of errors made by all students in each group.
- After reading the story, practice any difficult words.
- If the group has not reached the accuracy goal, have the group reread the story, mixing group and individual turns.

3. Repeated Readings

a. Partner Reading

During students' daily independent work, have them do Partner Reading.

b. Homework 1

Have students read the story at home. (A reprint of this story is available on a blackline master in *Read Well* Homework.)

---

in • sect = insect

CHAPTER 2

What did Fred learn about in Chapter 1?**1**

Fred's Frog Facts

Fred said, "Listen to my frog facts."

1. I was a frog egg.

Fish eat frog eggs. The fish did

not get me.

Fred was lucky. What does a fish do with frog eggs?**2**

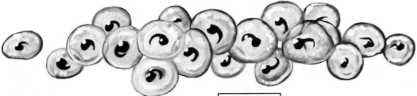

2. Then I was a .

You know facts about tadpoles.
What do you know about tadpoles?**3**

27

---

❶ **Summarizing** (Fred learned about metamorphosis. He learned how he began as an egg. He learned that he hatched into a tadpole, that he grew legs, and that he became a frog.)

❷ **Identifying—What** (A fish eats frog eggs.)

❸ **Identifying—Facts** (Tadpoles come from frog eggs and tadpoles grow up to be frogs.)

3. I got legs. My back legs are long and strong.

4. Soon, I was a frog. A frog eats insects. A fly can stick to my .

What do frogs eat?[1] How do frogs catch flies?[2]

Fred said, "I can think.
What am I thinking?
A frog eats insects.
So, I think I need to
eat an insect."

What does Fred think he should do?[3] Frogs love to eat—just like many other animals. In the next story, you'll learn about other things that frogs eat.[4]

28

[1] **Identifying—What** (A frog eats insects.)
[2] **Explaining** (Frogs catch flies with their tongues; insects stick to their tongues.)
[3] **Identifying—What** (Fred thinks he needs to eat an insect.)
[4] **Teacher Think Aloud**

COMPREHENSION BUILDING: FACT SUMMARY

Read the text. Have students look at the pictures and orally answer each question. If students have difficulty answering a question, discuss the pictures and/or reread the portion of the text from Chapters 1 and 2 that answer the question.

Fantastic Frog Facts[1]

We learned many facts about frogs. Look at the pictures and answer the questions with the facts you learned. What should you do if you can't answer a question?

What does a frog start out as?[2]

What does it become next?[3]

How does a tadpole breathe?[4]
What does the tadpole grow?[5]

What does a tadpole become?[6]

What are these changes called?[7]

What else do you know about frogs?[8]
What else would you like to learn about frogs?[9]

29

---

❶ Building Knowledge

❷ Identifying—What (A frog starts out as an egg.)

❸ Identifying—What (The egg becomes a tadpole.)

❹ Explaining (A tadpole breathes with gills.)

❺ Identifying—What (A tadpole grows legs.)

❻ Identifying—What (A tadpole becomes a frog.)

❼ Using Vocabulary (These changes are called metamorphosis.)

❽ Priming Background Knowledge, Making Connections

❾ Questioning

FACT SHEET

Use work pages from the workbook.

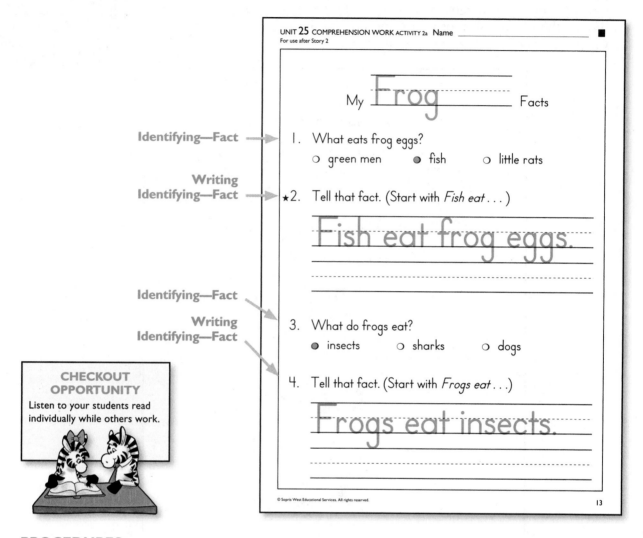

UNIT **25** COMPREHENSION WORK ACTIVITY 2a **Name** _____ ■
For use after Story 2

My <u>Frog</u> Facts

Identifying—Fact ⟶ 1. What eats frog eggs?
○ green men   ● fish   ○ little rats

Writing
Identifying—Fact ⟶ ★2. Tell that fact. (Start with *Fish eat* . . .)

Fish eat frog eggs.

Identifying—Fact
Writing
Identifying—Fact

3. What do frogs eat?
● insects   ○ sharks   ○ dogs

4. Tell that fact. (Start with *Frogs eat* . . .)

Frogs eat insects.

13

CHECKOUT OPPORTUNITY
Listen to your students read individually while others work.

PROCEDURES

For each step, demonstrate and guide practice as needed. Tell students that this fact sheet is about frogs. Have them write in the word "Frog" in the title, using a capital letter F.

1. Multiple Choice—Basic Instructions (Items 1, 3)

Have students fill in the bubble for the correct answer. Periodically, think aloud with students. Discuss the multiple choice options. As appropriate, ask questions like: "Does the first answer make sense?" "Is that what the book said?" "Is the answer completely correct?"

2. Sentence Writing—Specific Instructions (Items 2, 4)

★ • Have students read the direction and tell the fact using a complete sentence.

 • Have students write the complete sentence that starts with a capital letter and ends with a period.

ALPHABET DETECTIVE
Use work pages from the workbook.

CHECKOUT OPPORTUNITY
Listen to your students read individually while others work.

UNIT **25** SKILL WORK ACTIVITY 2b
ALPHABET DETECTIVE: For use after Story 2   Name _____

F f   g

F as in Frog

Capital letter F small letter f,

F says fff,

Funny flying frog,

F, f, fff.

14   © Sopris West Educational Services. All rights reserved.

PROCEDURES
For each step, demonstrate and guide practice as needed.

1. **Letter Find—Basic Instructions**
   - Have students look at the first box at the top of the page and follow the directions. Ask:

     What letters will you look for? (The capital letter F and the small letter f)

     What will you do when you find a capital letter F or a small letter f? (Draw a triangle around it.)

   - Have students look at the second box at the top of the page. Ask:

     What other letter will you look for? (The small letter g)

     What will you do when you find a small letter g? (Circle it.)

2. **Self-Monitoring—Basic Instructions**
   Have students systematically check each line after finishing the task.

   Alternative: At the beginning of the exercise, tell students the number of f's they will draw a triangle around, and the number of g's they will circle. Have students write the numbers on the top of their papers. When students complete the activity, have them count the number of triangles and circles they have drawn. If the numbers are incorrect, they can recheck each line.

3. **Coloring—Optional**
   Have students carefully color the picture, using at least three colors.

   Note: If students have difficulty with the multi-step directions, have them do just the first step.

① SOUND REVIEW

② NEW SOUND PRACTICE

◆◆ **③ FOCUS ON VOCABULARY**

Review vocabulary word: "metamorphosis"

- Have students review the word "metamorphosis." Clarify meaning. Say something like:

  Your vocabulary word is "metamorphosis." Tell me the word. (metamorphosis)

  A *metamorphosis* is a change. A caterpillar goes through a . . . (metamorphosis).

  When a tadpole becomes a frog, it's gone through a . . . (metamorphosis).

④ SOUNDING OUT SMOOTHLY

- For each word, have students say the underlined part, sound out the word, and then read the word.

  Use the words in sentences as needed.

- Provide repeated practice. Mix group and individual turns, independent of your voice.

⑤ MULTISYLLABIC WORDS

- Have students first *say* each of the word's parts and then read the whole word.
- If students have difficulty, have them *sound out* each of the word parts, then read each part, and then read the whole word.
- Repeat, mixing group and individual turns, independent of your voice. Use the words in sentences as needed.

◆◆ **⑥ ACCURACY AND FLUENCY BUILDING**

- For each column, have students say any underlined part, then read each word.
- Have students read the whole column.
- Repeat practice on each column, building accuracy first and then fluency.

Note: The sound pattern /-ing/ is relatively new. To build fluency, have students practice the words on Decoding Practice 4. Or, add a list of /-ing/ words to the board. Some words students can read are: "sing," "wing," "ring," "king," and "thing."

◆◆ **⑦ TRICKY WORDS**

★ **New Tricky Word: "work"**

- Have students try to sound out the new Tricky Word "work." Say something like:

  Look at your new word. It's a little tricky, but I think you can figure it out.

  Sound it out in your head, then keep it a secret until I count to five.

- Count to five and have students say the word.
- Have students read the row. Repeat, mixing group and individual turns, independent of your voice.

  Use the words in sentences as needed.

⑧ DAILY STORY READING

Proceed to the Unit 25 Storybook. See Daily Lesson Planning for pacing suggestions.

⑨ COMPREHENSION AND SKILL WORK ACTIVITY 3 AND/OR ACTIVITY 4

See pages 33 and/or 37.

UNIT **25** DECODING PRACTICE 2
(For use with Stories 3 and 4)

1. **SOUND REVIEW** Use Sound Cards for Units 1–25 or Sound Review on Decoding Practice 4.

2. **NEW SOUND PRACTICE** Have students read, trace, and say /fff/.

3. **FOCUS ON VOCABULARY** Review "metamorphosis."
See the Teacher's Guide for detailed instructions.

4. **SOUNDING OUT SMOOTHLY** For each word, have students say the underlined part, sound out the word in one smooth breath, and then read the word.

● Fr<u>a</u>n   cl<u>ea</u>n   f<u>oo</u>d   m<u>a</u>rsh   m<u>ea</u>l

5. **MULTISYLLABIC WORDS** Have students say each word part, then read the whole word.

■ fan·tas·tic = fantastic   near·by = nearby

6. **ACCURACY/FLUENCY BUILDING** For each column, have students say any underlined part, then read each word. Next, have students read the column.

▲	✈	✿
w<u>ing</u>s	Tank	green
think<u>ing</u>	thank	grin
sitt<u>ing</u>	think	fin
	thing	fins

★7. **TRICKY WORDS** Introduce "work" using the Tricky Word procedure. Next, have students silently figure out each word and then read it aloud.

♥ ★work   Look   so   two

8. DAILY STORY READING

6

Sentence Suggestions: Use the appropriate suggested sentence *after* decoding each individual word.

DUET STORY READING INSTRUCTIONS

Students read from their own storybooks.

The teacher reads the small text and students read the large text.

PACING

- 2- to 4-Day Plans: Have students do the first reading of Duet Story 3.

  Then proceed to repeated readings of Solo Story 4.

- 6- to 10-Day Plans: Have students do the first *and* second readings as needed.

COMPREHENSION BUILDING: DISCUSSION QUESTIONS AND TEACHER THINK ALOUDS

- Ask questions and discuss text on the first reading when indicated in the storybook in light gray text.

- Encourage students to answer questions with complete sentences when appropriate.

- If students have difficulty with a comprehension question, think aloud with them or reread the portion of the story that answers the question. Then, ask the question again.

PROCEDURES

1. First Reading

Mix group and individual turns on student-read sentences. On individual turns, gently correct any error, and then have the student reread the text.

2. Second Reading

Repeat the reading only as needed for comprehension.

Fred's Fish Tank

CHAPTER I
Captured

Fred was a big green bullfrog who lived in a marsh. All day long, Fred watched for scrumptious things to eat.

He hid in the weeds where it was cool and wet.

Fred didn't need to work. He sat in his marsh. When an insect would land nearby, Fred would eat it. When a fish swam by, Fred would eat it.

Where does the story begin?**1** Do you think Fred enjoys his life in the marsh?**2** What makes you think so?**3**

30

1 Identifying—Where (The story begins in a marsh.)

2 Inferring

3 Inferring, Explaining (The marsh was cool and wet; he could eat whatever he wanted.)

One summer day, Fran and her dad were exploring the edges of Fred's marsh. That was the day poor Fred was captured!

Fran said, "Look, Dad. I can see a big, green frog. He is sitting in the weeds." With a swoosh, Fred was in a net. Fred said, "I think this is bad."

VISUALIZING
Making Connections, Responding

After reading the page, say something like:

What happened to Fred? (He was caught in a net and put in a fish tank.)

Close your eyes. Imagine someone catching you in a net.

Now imagine being plopped into a fish tank. How would you feel?

What happened to Fred?**1**

Soon, Fred was sitting in Fran's fish tank. Life as Fred had known it had suddenly changed! When the journey ended, Fred found himself sitting in a fish tank.

How do you think Fred will like his new life in the fish tank?**2**

31

❶ **Explaining** (He was caught in a net.)
❷ **Predicting**

STORY COMPREHENSION

Use work pages from the workbook.

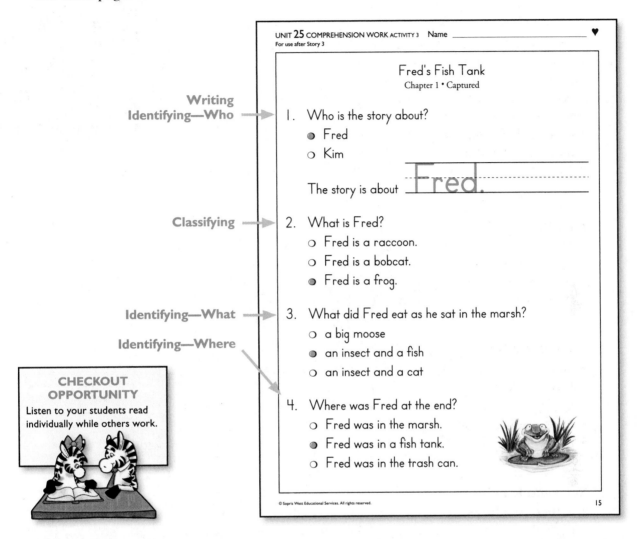

Writing
Identifying—Who

Classifying

Identifying—What

Identifying—Where

CHECKOUT OPPORTUNITY

Listen to your students read individually while others work.

UNIT **25** COMPREHENSION WORK ACTIVITY 3   Name _____   ♥
For use after Story 3

Fred's Fish Tank
Chapter 1 • Captured

1. Who is the story about?
   ● Fred
   ○ Kim

   The story is about ___Fred.___

2. What is Fred?
   ○ Fred is a raccoon.
   ○ Fred is a bobcat.
   ● Fred is a frog.

3. What did Fred eat as he sat in the marsh?
   ○ a big moose
   ● an insect and a fish
   ○ an insect and a cat

4. Where was Fred at the end?
   ○ Fred was in the marsh.
   ● Fred was in a fish tank.
   ○ Fred was in the trash can.

© Sopris West Educational Services. All rights reserved.   15

PROCEDURES

For each step, demonstrate and guide practice as needed.

1. Multiple Choice, Sentence Completion—Basic Instructions (Item 1)
- Have students fill in the bubble for the correct answer.
- Have them write an answer in the blank and place a period at the end.

2. Multiple Choice—Basic Instructions (Items 2, 3, 4)
Have students fill in the bubble for the correct answer. Periodically, think aloud with students. Discuss the multiple choice options. As appropriate, ask questions like: "Does the first answer make sense?" "Is that what the book said?" "Is the answer completely correct?"

SOLO STORY READING INSTRUCTIONS

Students read from their own storybooks.

COMPREHENSION BUILDING:
DISCUSSION QUESTIONS AND TEACHER THINK ALOUDS

- Ask questions and discuss text on the first reading when indicated in the storybook in light gray text.
- Encourage students to answer questions with complete sentences when appropriate.
- If students have difficulty with a comprehension question, think aloud with them or reread the portion of the story that answers the question. Then, ask the question again.

PROCEDURES

1. First Reading

- Mix group and individual turns on student-read sentences. On individual turns, gently correct any error, and then have the student reread the text.
- After students complete the first reading and before the second reading, have students practice a paragraph. First demonstrate expressive reading for students, then give individual turns. Acknowledge student efforts.

2. Second Reading

- Mix group and individual turns, independent of your voice. Have students work toward an accuracy goal of 0–2 errors. Quietly keep track of errors made by all students in each group.
- After reading the story, practice any difficult words.
- If the group has not reached the accuracy goal, have the group reread the story, mixing group and individual turns.

3. Repeated Readings
a. Timed Readings

- Once the accuracy goal has been achieved, have individual students read the page while the other children track the text with their fingers and whisper read.

  Time individuals for 30 seconds and encourage each student to work for a personal best.
- Count the number of words read correctly in 30 seconds (words read minus errors). Multiply by two to determine words correct per minute. Record student scores.

b. Partner Reading

During students' daily independent work, have them do Partner Reading.

c. Homework 2

Have students read the story at home. (A reprint of this story is available on a blackline master in *Read Well* Homework.)

STORY 4, SOLO

CHAPTER 2
In the Tank

Who is the story about?**1** What happened to Fred in the last chapter?**2**

Fred sat in Fran's fish tank. He was thinking, "Where is my meal?"

Fran said, "Big, green frog! Look! This meal has 6 legs and two wings."

With that, Fred had an insect meal. Fred began to think, "Well, well. This isn't too bad."

Why was Fred thinking life in the fish tank wasn't so bad?**3**

32

❶ Summarizing, Identifying—Who (The story is about Fred.)

❷ Summarizing, Identifying—Action (He got caught and put in a fish tank.)

❸ Inferring, Explaining (Fran brought him food.)

Soon Fran was back. She said, "This meal has gills and fins."

With that, Fred had a fish to eat. Fred began to think. "This tank is clean and wet. I get fantastic food. Not bad! Not so bad at all!"

Name two things that Fred liked about the fish tank. **I**

FOCUS ON EXPRESSION

After the first reading and before the second reading, practice paragraphs to develop expression. Select a paragraph. Demonstrate expressive reading, then provide group and/or individual turns. Say something like:

In the last paragraph, how was Fred feeling about his life in the fish tank?

I think he was happy, a little surprised, and satisfied. Listen to me read. I'm going to make Fred sound happy, surprised, and satisfied.

Now it's your turn.

33

❶ **Identifying** (The tank was clean and wet; he got fantastic food.)

STORY COMPREHENSION

Use work pages from the workbook.

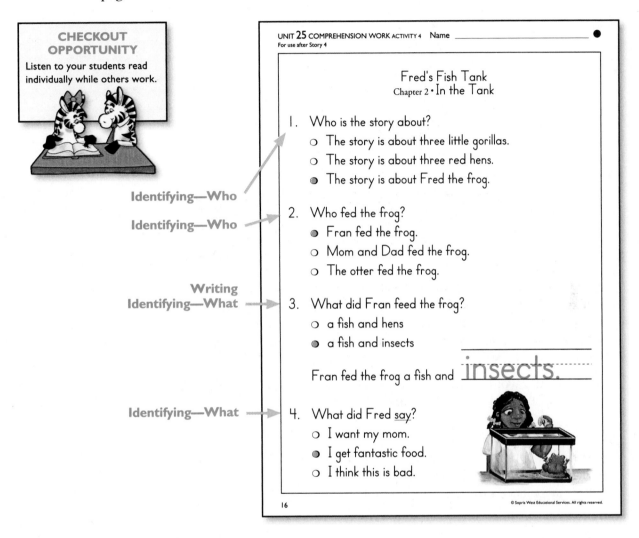

CHECKOUT OPPORTUNITY

Listen to your students read individually while others work.

Identifying—Who

Identifying—Who

Writing
Identifying—What

Identifying—What

UNIT **25** COMPREHENSION WORK ACTIVITY 4   Name _____
For use after Story 4

Fred's Fish Tank
Chapter 2 • In the Tank

1. Who is the story about?
    ○ The story is about three little gorillas.
    ○ The story is about three red hens.
    ● The story is about Fred the frog.

2. Who fed the frog?
    ● Fran fed the frog.
    ○ Mom and Dad fed the frog.
    ○ The otter fed the frog.

3. What did Fran feed the frog?
    ○ a fish and hens
    ● a fish and insects

    Fran fed the frog a fish and <u>insects.</u>

4. What did Fred <u>say</u>?
    ○ I want my mom.
    ● I get fantastic food.
    ○ I think this is bad.

16

PROCEDURES

For each step, demonstrate and guide practice as needed.

1. Multiple Choice—Basic Instructions (Items 1, 2, 4)

Have students fill in the bubble for the correct answer. Periodically, think aloud with students. Discuss the multiple choice options. As appropriate, ask questions like: "Does the first answer make sense?" "Is that what the book said?" "Is the answer completely correct?"

2. Multiple Choice, Sentence Completion—Basic Instructions (Item 3)

- Have students select and fill in the bubble next to the words that correctly complete the sentence.
- Have them write an answer in the blank and place a period at the end.

① SOUND REVIEW

Use selected Sound Cards from Units 1–25 or the Sound Review on Decoding Practice 4.

② NEW SOUND PRACTICE

◆◆ ③ FOCUS ON VOCABULARY

- Have students use the word "metamorphosis." Say something like:

  A metamorphosis is a . . . change.

  The caterpillar changed into a butterfly. It went through a . . . (metamorphosis).

  The tadpole changed into a frog. It went through a . . . (metamorphosis).

◆◆ ④ SOUNDING OUT SMOOTHLY

- For each word, have students sound out the word and then read the word. Use the words in sentences as needed.
- Provide repeated practice. Mix group and individual turns, independent of your voice.

⑤ MULTISYLLABIC WORDS

- Have students first *say* each of the word's parts and then read the whole word.
- If students have difficulty, have them *sound out* each of the word parts, then read each part, and then read the whole word.
- Repeat, mixing group and individual turns, independent of your voice. Use the words in sentences as needed.

Note: For the word "insects," you may want to use a procedure similar to the one suggested for "facts." Remind students that the t in "listen" is silent.

◆◆ ⑥ ACCURACY AND FLUENCY BUILDING

- For each column, have students say any underlined part, then read each word.
- Have students read the whole column.
- Repeat practice on each column, building accuracy first and then fluency.

⑦ TRICKY WORDS

Have students read the row. Repeat, mixing group and individual turns, independent of your voice.

Use the words in sentences as needed.

⑧ DAILY STORY READING

Proceed to the Unit 25 Storybook. See Daily Lesson Planning for pacing suggestions.

⑨ COMPREHENSION AND SKILL WORK ACTIVITY 5 AND/OR ACTIVITY 6

See pages 45 and/or 49, 50.

UNIT **25** DECODING PRACTICE 3
(For use with Stories 5 and 6)

1. SOUND REVIEW Use Sound Cards for Units 1–25 or Sound Review on Decoding Practice 4.

2. NEW SOUND PRACTICE Have students read, trace, and say /fff/.

3. FOCUS ON VOCABULARY Review "metamorphosis." See the Teacher's Guide for detailed instructions.

4. SOUNDING OUT SMOOTHLY Have students sound out each word in one smooth breath and then read the word.

■   best   If   fast   nodded

5. MULTISYLLABIC WORDS Have students say each word part, then read the whole word.

| ● | be·gan = began | in·sects = insects |
| ▲ | lis·ten = listen | lit·tle = little |

6. ACCURACY/FLUENCY BUILDING For each column, have students say any underlined part, then read each word. Next, have students read the column.

✈	✎	■■	✿
fat	let	gill	sang
frog	lot	fill	song
feed	log	fell	sing

7. TRICKY WORDS Have students silently figure out each word and then read it aloud.

♥   legs   eggs   work   go

8. DAILY STORY READING

7

◆◆ **SENTENCE SUGGESTIONS**

■ best – We are a team. We will do our *best*. What will we do?

■ If – *If* you are happy and you know it, smile.

■ fast – A [jet] moves *fast*. How does a [jet] move?

✈ fat – Fred was a *fat* frog. What kind of frog was Fred?

✿ sing – The frog likes to *sing*.

♥ work – We *work* hard. What do we do? (We *work* hard.)

Sentence Suggestions: Use the appropriate suggested sentence *after* decoding each individual word.

DUET STORY READING INSTRUCTIONS

Students read from their own storybooks.

The teacher reads the small text and students read the large text.

PACING

- 2- to 4-Day Plans: Have students do the first reading of Duet Story 5.
  Then proceed to repeated readings of Solo Story 6.
- 6- to 10-Day Plans: Have students do the first *and* second readings as needed.

COMPREHENSION BUILDING:
DISCUSSION QUESTIONS AND TEACHER THINK ALOUDS

- Ask questions and discuss text on the first reading when indicated in the storybook in light gray text.
- Encourage students to answer questions with complete sentences when appropriate.
- If students have difficulty with a comprehension question, think aloud with them or reread the portion of the story that answers the question. Then, ask the question again.

PROCEDURES

1. First Reading

Mix group and individual turns on student-read sentences. On individual turns, gently correct any error, and then have the student reread the text.

2. Second Reading

Repeat the reading only as needed for comprehension.

3. Summarizing and Inferring

Have students review who and what the story is about. Say something like:
This is Chapter 3 of "Fred's Fish Tank." Who is the main character? (Fred)
What happened to Fred? (He got caught in a net and put in a fish tank.)
What did Fred think of that? (He thought it wasn't so bad.)

CHAPTER 3

A Night With Fred

Who is the story about?[1] What happened to Fred?[2]

The day Fred was captured, Fran's dad had said. "Fran, are you sure you want to take that bullfrog home? It is a big responsibility."
What does Fran's dad mean?[3]

Dad had said, "That big frog will need to eat a lot."

Fran said, "I can feed the frog insects and fish to eat."

So, that is what Fran did.

All day long, Fran ran from here to there finding flies and catching fish. Fred was happy to sit and wait for his food. By night, Fred was full and Fran was exhausted. Her head had barely touched her pillow when . . .

What do you think is going to happen next?[4]

34

❶ **Summarizing, Identifying—Who** (The story is about Fred.)

❷ **Summarizing—Action** (He was captured and put in a fish tank.)

❸ **Inferring, Explaining**

❹ **Predicting**

Fred began to sing. Fred had a beautiful

deep voice. "Arroooom." Fred loved to hear his own voice. "Arroooom, arroooom."

What did Fred sing?[1]

Fred said, "Listen to me. I can sing." Then the fat frog sat in his fish tank and sang and sang.

How long do you think Fred sang?[2] What problem do you think Fran had?[3]

35

❶ **Identifying—What** (Arrooom, arrooom)

❷ **Inferring** (It looks like he sang all night long.)

❸ **Inferring—Problem** (Fran couldn't sleep.)

STORY 5, DUET

Soon it was morning. Fred sat happily resting in his fish tank. He thought, "I wonder what's for breakfast." But before he knew it, Fred was back in the car.

Where do you think Fran was taking Fred?**1**

In the car, Fran said, "I think this is best. There are fish and insects in the marsh. I think it is best to let the frog go."

Why do you think Fran decided to let Fred go?**2**

Fran's dad nodded.

Before Fred knew it, he was back in his marsh. It was wet and cool. Fred said, "What's to eat?" With that a fish swam by and Fred had a fine fish meal.

Soon Fred was singing again. "Arroooom, arroooom, arroooom."

Why was Fred happy in the marsh?**3**Do you think Fred was happy in the fish tank?**4**Why?**5**I wonder if Fred even remembers when he lived in the fish tank.**6** What do you think?**7**

36

❶ **Predicting** (She was taking him back to the marsh.)

❷ **Inferring, Explaining** (It was hard to feed him; he was too noisy at night.)

❸ **Inferring** (It was wet and cool; he could eat what he wanted.)

❹ **Inferring**

❺ **Inferring, Explaining**

❻ **Teacher Think Aloud**

❼ **Inferring**

COMPREHENSION BUILDING: ORAL STORY RETELL

- Have students study the pictures, then ask questions and discuss the pictures as indicated in the storybook in light gray text. The circle, square, and triangle provide visual references for the beginning, middle, and end of the story.

STORY SUMMARY

Fred's Fish Tank

We're going to retell "Fred's Fish Tank."[1]
What was the title of the story?[2]
Look the pictures.
Who was the story about?[3]

● At the beginning of the story, where was Fred?[4]
What was he doing?[5]

■ In the middle of the story, what had happened to Fred?[6]

▲ At the end of the story, where was Fred?[7]
What was Fred doing?[8]

Let's go back to the beginning and retell the whole story by looking at the pictures. Look at the first picture. This story was about . . .[9]

37

❶ **Summarizing, Sequencing**

❷ **Identifying—Title** (The title of the story was "Fred's Fish Tank.")

❸ **Identifying—Who** (The story was about Fred.)

❹ **Explaining—Beginning, Identifying—Where** (At the beginning of the story Fred was in a marsh.)

❺ **Identifying—Action** (He was eating insects and fish.)

❻ **Explaining—Middle, Action** (In the middle of the story, Fran caught Fred and put him in a fish tank. Then Fran fed Fred insects and fish.)

❼ **Explaining—End, Identifying—Where** (At the end of the story, Fred was back in the marsh.)

❽ **Explaining—Action** (Fred was eating a fish and singing.)

❾ **Summarizing, Sequencing**

STORY MAP

Use work pages from the workbook.

Sequencing

**Explaining—Beginning
Writing
Identifying—Who, What**

**Explaining—Middle
Writing
Identifying—What**

**Explaining—End
Writing
Identifying—Where**

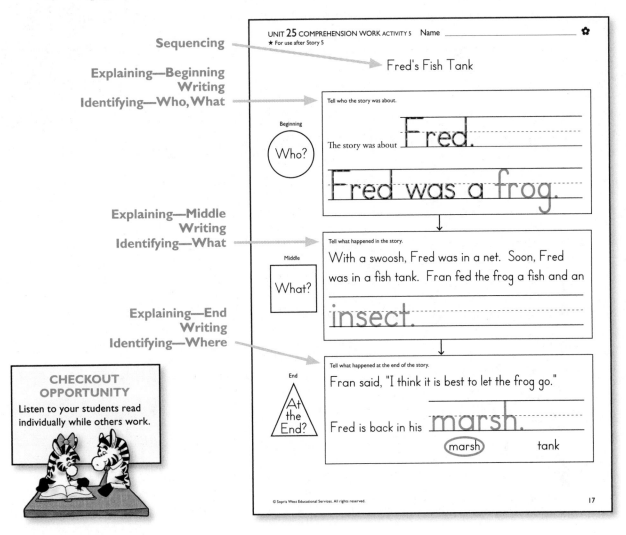

UNIT **25** COMPREHENSION WORK ACTIVITY 5   Name _____
★ For use after Story 5

Fred's Fish Tank

Beginning

(Who?)

Tell who the story was about.

The story was about Fred.

Fred was a frog.

Middle

[What?]

Tell what happened in the story.

With a swoosh, Fred was in a net. Soon, Fred was in a fish tank. Fran fed the frog a fish and an

insect.

End

△ At
the
End?

Tell what happened at the end of the story.

Fran said, "I think it is best to let the frog go."

Fred is back in his marsh.

(marsh)   tank

© Sopris West Educational Services. All rights reserved.   17

**CHECKOUT
OPPORTUNITY**

Listen to your students read
individually while others work.

PROCEDURES

For each step, demonstrate and guide practice as needed.

Story Map—Basic Instructions

- Using a blank or overhead copy of the story map, help students identify the basic story elements—who the story is about, what happened in the story, and what happened at the end.
- Have students fill in the blanks to create a story map of "Fred's Fish Tank."
- Remind students that a story map helps them retell or summarize the important parts of a story.

Note: You may wish to remind students that a sentence ends with a period.

SOLO STORY READING INSTRUCTIONS
Students read from their own storybooks.

POEM
Tell students that a poem is like a song. Explain that each part is called a verse.

PROCEDURES

1. First Reading
- Mix group and individual turns on student-read sentences. On individual turns, gently correct any error, and then have the student reread the text.
- After students read a verse, have students find the rhyming words. Repeat the verse with a poetic (but not sing-songy) cadence.

2. Repeated Readings
a. Repeat Verses to Fluency
- Have students choral read a verse.
- Practice any difficult words.
- Demonstrate or guide practice, gradually increasing fluency.
Repeat with each verse.

b. Partner Reading

During students' daily independent work, have them do Partner Reading.

c. Homework 3

Have students read the story at home. (A reprint of this story is available on a blackline master in *Read Well* Homework.)

sing   sang   song

Three Frogs on a Log

Fred was a big fat frog,

Who sat on a big fat log.

"Hear my song," said Fred to Bill.

Then he sang and Bill sat still.

38

47

Bill was a small fat frog,

Who sat on that big long log.

"See my trick," said Bill to Nick.

Then Bill began to kick, kick, kick.

Nick was the last green frog,

Who sat on that big strong log.

"Fred," said Bill, "See Nick swim.

See Nick swim to little Kim."

39

48

STORY COMPREHENSION

Use work pages from the workbook.

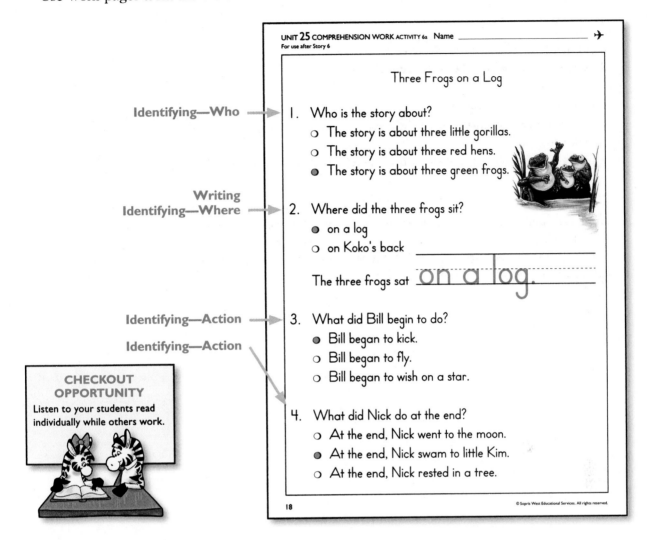

Identifying—Who

Writing
Identifying—Where

Identifying—Action

Identifying—Action

CHECKOUT OPPORTUNITY
Listen to your students read individually while others work.

UNIT **25** COMPREHENSION WORK ACTIVITY 6a   Name _____
For use after Story 6

Three Frogs on a Log

1. Who is the story about?
    o The story is about three little gorillas.
    o The story is about three red hens.
    ● The story is about three green frogs.

2. Where did the three frogs sit?
    ● on a log
    o on Koko's back

    The three frogs sat on a log.

3. What did Bill begin to do?
    ● Bill began to kick.
    o Bill began to fly.
    o Bill began to wish on a star.

4. What did Nick do at the end?
    o At the end, Nick went to the moon.
    ● At the end, Nick swam to little Kim.
    o At the end, Nick rested in a tree.

18   © Sopris West Educational Services. All rights reserved.

PROCEDURES

For each step, demonstrate and guide practice as needed.

1. Multiple Choice—Basic Instructions (Items 1, 3, 4)

Have students fill in the bubble for the correct answer. Periodically, think aloud with students. Discuss the multiple choice options. As appropriate, ask questions like: "Does the first answer make sense?" "Is that what the book said?" "Is the answer completely correct?"

2. Multiple Choice, Sentence Completion—Basic Instructions (Item 2)

• Have students select and fill in the bubble next to the words that correctly complete the sentence.
• Have them write the answer in the blank and place a period at the end.

RHYMING PATTERNS

Use work pages from the workbook.

PROCEDURES

Demonstrate and guide practice as needed.

Rhyming Patterns—Basic Instructions

For each box, have students:

- Read the rhyming pattern.
- Circle the two sounds above the rhyming pattern that go with it to make real words.
- Cross out the sound that does not make a real word with the rhyming pattern.
- Write the two rhyming words on the lines provided.

Note: For students who struggle or who lack the English language base to know which are real words, you may wish to identify the two sounds they should circle in each box. Students can then write the pattern words on their own.

UNIT 25 SKILL WORK ACTIVITY 6b
RHYMING PATTERNS: For use after Story 6

Name _____ ✈

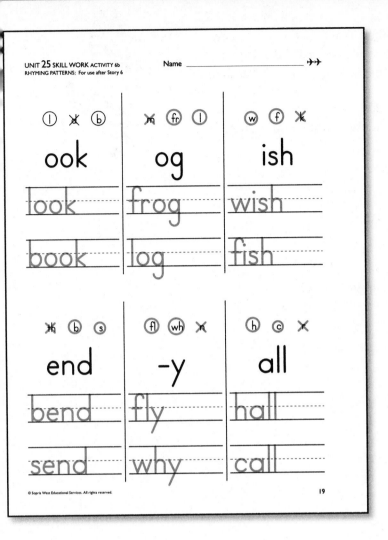

ⓛ ⓧ ⓑ   ⓝ ⓕⓡ ⓛ   ⓦ ⓕ ⓧ

ook   **og**   **ish**

look   frog   wish

book   log   fish

ⓜ ⓑ ⓢ   ⓕⓛ ⓦⓗ ⓝ   ⓗ ⓒ ⓧ

end   **-y**   **all**

bend   fly   hall

send   why   call

19

Note: There are multiple uses for Decoding Practice 4.
- Use the Sound Review rows in place of Sound Card Practice.
- Use the whole page at the end of the unit for fluency building and/or to informally assess skills.
- Have students complete the page as a partner review.
- Build spelling dictation lessons from the sounds and words on this page.

① SOUND REVIEW

② ACCURACY AND FLUENCY BUILDING

③ TRICKY WORDS

④ MULTISYLLABIC CHALLENGE WORDS

⑤ DAILY STORY READING
See Daily Lesson Planning for story suggestions.

WHOLE CLASS VARIATION
Put a couple of rows or columns on the board and have the whole class practice the sounds and/or words.

UNIT **25** DECODING PRACTICE 4
(See Daily Lesson Planning for story suggestions.)

1. SOUND REVIEW Demonstrate an appropriate pace. Have students read the sounds in each row.

■	f	o	wh	G	–y	K	ee	7
✿	b	R	e	sh	F	oo	h	14
♥	c	i	g	ea	n	D	ar	21

2. ACCURACY/FLUENCY BUILDING For each column, have students say any underlined part, then read each word. Next, have students read the column.

✈	✈✈	✿	✿✿	✿✿✿
fr<u>o</u>g	c<u>all</u>	fly	sang	f<u>i</u>t
hog	tall	fry	rang	f<u>a</u>t
dog	small	free	ring	f<u>ee</u>t
log	ball	tree	bring	f<u>ee</u>d
bog	fall	three	sing	f<u>oo</u>d

3. TRICKY WORDS Have students silently figure out each word and then read it aloud.

☆☆	What	should	no	two	there
☆☆	about	want	one	has	legs

4. MULTISYLLABIC CHALLENGE WORDS Have students say each word part, then read the whole word.

fin·ish = finish	fif·teen = fifteen
fan·tas·tic = fantastic	soft·ball = softball

5. DAILY STORY READING

8

**THE REWARDS
OF HARD WORK**
**Help students
recognize their
accomplishments.**
Students may lose sight of
the amount of progress
they've made. Compare
Decoding Practice 4 from
Unit 2 with Decoding
Practice 4 from Unit 25.

End of the Unit

In this section, you will find:

Making Decisions

As you near the end of the unit, you will need to make decisions. Should you administer the Oral Reading Fluency Assessment or should you teach Extra Practice lessons?

Unit 25 Oral Reading Fluency Assessment

The Unit 25 Oral Reading Fluency Assessment is located on page 56 and can also be found in the *Assessment Manual*.

Certificate of Achievement

Celebrate your children's accomplishments.

Extra Practice

Lessons and blackline masters for added decoding practice and independent work are provided for students who need extended practice opportunities.

Making Decisions

ASSESSMENT READINESS

Assess when students are able to easily complete decoding tasks from the beginning of a lesson.

- If you aren't sure whether students are ready for the assessment, give the assessment. Do Extra Practice lessons if needed.
- If students are not ready for the assessment, proceed to Extra Practice lessons. Administer the assessment as soon as students are ready.

GENERAL ASSESSMENT GUIDELINES

- Assess all students.
- Assess each child individually.
- Score student responses on the Student Assessment Record, adhering to the scoring criteria in the *Assessment Manual*. Use a stopwatch to time how long it takes the student to read the oral fluency passage.
- Follow the general instructions at the bottom of each assessment. Record a Strong Pass, a Weak Pass, or a No Pass.

ACCELERATION

- If students read with 100% accuracy and exceed the fluency goal, consider shortening units.
- If an individual student reads with greater fluency than others in his or her group, consider regrouping.

ASSESSING UNPRACTICED READING (Reminder)

Do not have children practice the assessments. The goal of reading instruction is to provide children with the skills to read independently.

INTERVENTION OPTIONS—INDIVIDUALS

1. Add informal practice throughout the day.
2. Add practice with repeated readings on Solo Stories.
3. Find ways to provide a double dose of Read Well instruction.
4. Consider placement in a lower group. If one child's fluency scores are significantly lower than the other children in the group, success will be impossible without additional and intensive practice.

INTERVENTION OPTIONS—GROUP

1. Extend the unit with Extra Practice lessons.
2. Consider a Jell-Well Review before moving forward. (See the *Assessment Manual*.)

CERTIFICATE OF ACHIEVEMENT

When students pass the assessment, celebrate with the Certificate of Achievement. Then, set a personal goal. (See *Getting Started*.)

TRICKY WORD WARM-UP

work	about	eggs	no	who

ORAL READING FLUENCY PASSAGE

Go, Fly, Go

★There was a big fly in my room. It had   10

long wings. It landed on my fish tank.   18

Fred said, "The fish will eat that fly."   26

So I said, "Get off, fly." The fly was foolish.   36

He fell into the fish tank because he went   45

too fast.   47

ORAL READING FLUENCY	Start timing at the ★. Mark errors. Make a single slash in the text (/) at 60 seconds. Have student complete passage. If the student completes the passage in less than 60 seconds, have the student go back to the ★ and continue reading. Make a double slash (//) in the text at 60 seconds.
WCPM	Determine words correct per minute by subtracting errors from words read in 60 seconds.
STRONG PASS	The student scores no more than 2 errors on the first pass through the passage and reads a minimum of 60 or more words correct per minute. Proceed to Unit 26.
WEAK PASS	The student scores no more than 2 errors on the first pass through the passage and reads 46 to 59 words correct per minute. Proceed to Unit 26 with added fluency practice, or provide Extra Practice lessons in Unit 25, and/or provide a Jell-Well Review.
NO PASS	The student scores 3 or more errors on the first pass through the passage and/or reads 45 or fewer words correct per minute. Provide Extra Practice lessons and retest, and/or provide a Jell-Well Review.

Certificate of Achievement

This certifies that

_____,

on this _____ day of _____, _____,

has successfully completed

Read Well Unit 25

Sounds Mastered: s, e, ee, m, a, d, th, n, t, w, i, Th, h, c, r, ea, sh, k, -ck, oo, ar, wh, ĕ, -y (as in "fly"), l, o, b, all, g, f

Known Words: By Unit 24, you had learned and practiced 488 words.

New Words Mastered in Unit 25: egg, eggs, legs, work, call, dog, facts, fall, fantastic, fast, fat, feed, feet, fell, fifteen, fill, fin, finish, fins, fish, fit, fly, food, Fran, Fran's, Fred, Fred's, free, frog, frogs, fry, gill, gills, hog, if, insect, insects, log, marsh, meal, nearby, rang, ring, sang, sitting, softball, song, thinking, wings

You can now read 537 words—plus many other words made up of the sounds and patterns you've learned.

Note: Personal and Team Goal Setting forms can be copied from Units 16 and 17, or from *Getting Started*.

1 SOUNDS

Have students say each sound.

2 WORD DICTATION

Have students count the sounds in each word with their fingers, identify and write each sound, and then read the word. Use the words in sentences as needed.

fly, fast, fell, frog

The first word is "fly." We're going to count the sounds in "fly."
Tell me the first sound. **Hold up one finger.** (/fff/)
Repeat with /lll/ and /-yyy/.
How many sounds are in "fly"? (Three)

Tell me the first sound. (/fff/) Write it.
Repeat with /lll/ and /-yyy/.
Do Smooth Blending. (/fffllllyyy/) Read the word. (fly)

Repeat with "fast," "fell," and "frog."

DICTATION
• Demonstrate and guide practice as needed.
• Have students check and correct.

3 SENTENCE COMPLETION

The fly was *fast*.

• Have students read the beginning of the sentence with you.
• Dictate the last word "fast."
• Have students trace the dotted words and complete the sentence with a period.
• Have students read the sentence.

4 ACCURACY AND FLUENCY BUILDING

Repeat practice on each column, building accuracy first and then fluency.

5 TRICKY WORDS

Repeat practice, mixing group and individual turns, independent of your voice.

6 DAILY STORY READING

1. First Reading

Have students choral read Fluency Passage 1.

2. Second Reading

• Provide individual turns on sentences. Quietly keep track of errors.
• After reading, practice any difficult words.

3. Repeated Readings

a. Timed Readings

 • Have individual students read the passage while other students track the text with their fingers and whisper read. Time individuals for 30 seconds and encourage each student to work for a personal best.

• For each student, determine words correct per minute. Record students' scores.

b. Partner Reading—Checkout Opportunity

 While students are partner reading, listen to individuals read the passage.

Name_____

1. SOUNDS Have students say each sound.

| f | g | i | L | ea | b | o | G |

| e | r | -y | Wh | oo | F | a | ck |

2. WORD DICTATION Have students count the sounds in each word, identify and write each sound, and then read the word: "fly," "fast," "fell," and "frog."

1 _____   2 _____   3 _____   4 _____

3. SENTENCE COMPLETION Have students read the beginning of the sentence. Dictate "fast." Have students trace the words and complete the sentence with a period.

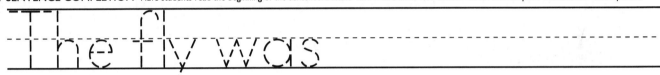
The fly was

4. ACCURACY/FLUENCY BUILDING In each column, have students say any underlined part, then read each word. Next, have students read the column.

♥	♥♥	♥♥♥
facts	off	<u>wante</u>d
fast	on	<u>foo</u>lish
fist	long	<u>lande</u>d
fish	wing	<u>fi</u>nish
fool	sing	<u>starte</u>d

5. TRICKY WORDS For each word, have students silently figure out the word, then read it aloud.

| work | Look | eggs | would | No |

6. DAILY STORY READING

Name_____

FLUENCY PASSAGE

Frogs Can't Fly	
When Fred was a little frog, he said,	8
"I want to fly."	12
His mom said, "Frogs can't fly. If we	20
had wings, we could fly."	25
Fred said, "I can't fly, but I can swim	34
and sing. So, I am not sad."	41

Have students read the sentences. Time individual students for 30 seconds; mark errors. To determine words correct per minute (wcpm), count words read in 30 seconds, subtract errors, multiply times two, and record on the chart. If student completes the passage in less than 30 seconds, have him or her return to the top and continue reading. (Repeated readings may be completed with older students, assistants, or parents.)

My goal is to read with 0–2 errors. This is what I did:

Reading	1st	2nd	3rd	4th
Errors				
Words/ 30 seconds				
wcpm				

60

Take-Home Game

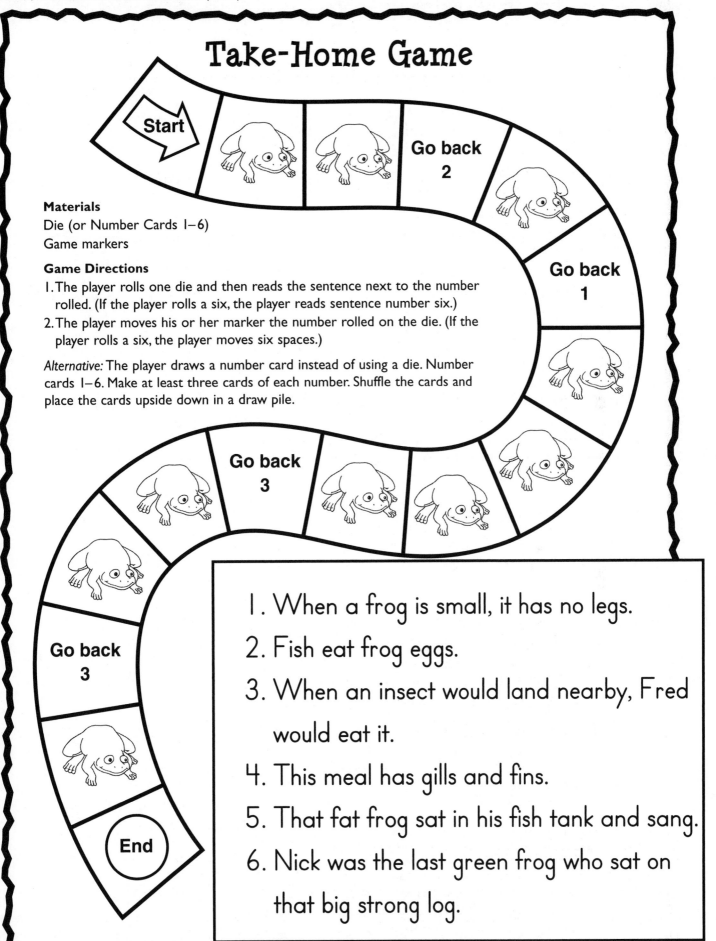

Materials
Die (or Number Cards 1–6)
Game markers

Game Directions
1. The player rolls one die and then reads the sentence next to the number rolled. (If the player rolls a six, the player reads sentence number six.)
2. The player moves his or her marker the number rolled on the die. (If the player rolls a six, the player moves six spaces.)

Alternative: The player draws a number card instead of using a die. Number cards 1–6. Make at least three cards of each number. Shuffle the cards and place the cards upside down in a draw pile.

Start

Go back
2

Go back
1

Go back
3

Go back
3

End

1. When a frog is small, it has no legs.
2. Fish eat frog eggs.
3. When an insect would land nearby, Fred would eat it.
4. This meal has gills and fins.
5. That fat frog sat in his fish tank and sang.
6. Nick was the last green frog who sat on that big strong log.

① **SOUNDS**

② **WORD DICTATION**

Have students count the sounds in each word with their fingers, identify and write each sound, and then read the word. Use the words in sentences as needed.

too, room, went, tank

The first word is "too." We're going to count the sounds in "too."
Tell me the first sound. **Hold up one finger.** (/t/)
Tell me the next sound. **Hold up two fingers.** (/oooo/)
How many sounds are in "too"? (Two)

Tell me the first sound. (/t/) Write it.
Tell me the next sound. (/oooo/) Write it with two <u>o</u>'s.
Do Smooth Blending. (/toooo/) Read the word. (too)

Repeat with "room," "went," and "tank."

HAVE STUDENTS CHECK AND CORRECT.

③ **SENTENCE COMPLETION**

***Fred* will eat fish.**

• Dictate and have students write the first word "Fred." Remind students to begin the first word of the sentence with a capital letter.
• Have students read and then trace the dotted words to complete the sentence.
• Have students read the sentence.

④ **ACCURACY AND FLUENCY BUILDING**

• Repeat practice on each column, building accuracy first and then fluency.

⑤ **TRICKY WORDS**

Repeat practice, mixing group and individual turns, independent of your voice.

⑥ **DAILY STORY READING**

1. First and Second Readings, Fluency Passage 2a
• Have students choral read the text.
• Provide individual turns on sentences. Quietly keep track of errors.
• After reading, practice any difficult words.

2. First and Second Readings, Fluency Passage 2b
Repeat step 1 with Fluency Passage 2b.

3. Repeated Readings
 a. Timed Readings
 • Have individual students read either passage 2a or 2b while other students track the text with their fingers and whisper read. Time individuals for 30 seconds and encourage each student to work for a personal best.

• For each student, determine words correct per minute. Record students' scores.

 **b. Partner Reading—
 Checkout Opportunity**
 While students are partner reading, listen to individuals read a passage.

UNIT 25 EXTRA PRACTICE 2 Name________________________

1. SOUNDS Have students say each sound.

F	-y	G	ee	k	ar	R	e
b	o	g	f	oo	D	h	i

2. WORD DICTATION Have students count the sounds in each word, identify and write each sound, and then read the word: "too," "room," "went," and "tank."

1 ____________ 2 ____________ 3 ____________ 4 ____________

3. SENTENCE COMPLETION Dictate and have students write "Fred." Have students read and then trace the words to complete the sentence.

____________ will eat fish.

4. ACCURACY/FLUENCY BUILDING In each column, have students say any underlined part, then read each word. Next, have students read the column.

♥	♥♥	♥♥♥
fly	Go	fit
fry	No	fat
free	Not	feet
tree	Got	feed
three	Get	food

5. TRICKY WORDS For each word, have students silently figure out the word, then read it aloud.

about who because was into

6. DAILY STORY READING

Name_____

FLUENCY PASSAGE A

Big Fred	
Big Fred sat in the marsh on a log.	9
He said, "I am hot. I think I need a	19
swim."	20

FLUENCY PASSAGE B

Swim, Fred, Swim	
Fred slid into the wet marsh because	7
he wanted to swim. Soon Fred said,	14
"That was great. I feel fantastic!"	20

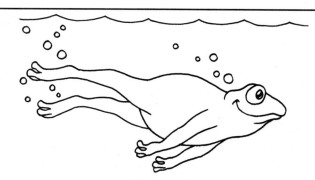

Have students read the sentences. Time individual students for 30 seconds; mark errors. To determine words correct per minute (wcpm), count words read in 30 seconds, subtract errors, multiply times two, and record on the chart. If student completes the passage in less than 30 seconds, have him or her return to the top and continue reading. (Repeated readings may be completed with older students, assistants, or parents.)

My goal is to read with 0–2 errors. This is what I did:

Reading	1st	2nd	3rd	4th
Errors				
Words/ 30 seconds				
wcpm				

64

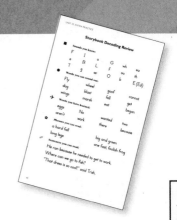

❶ STORYBOOK DECODING REVIEW

For each row, mix group and individual turns, independent of your voice.

❷ WORD DICTATION

Have students count the sounds in each word with their fingers, identify and write each sound, and then read the word. Use the words in sentences as needed.

fell, fly, my, get

The first word is "fell." We're going to count the sounds in "fell."
Tell me the first sound. **Hold up one finger.** (/fff/)
Repeat with /ĕĕĕ/ and /llll/.
How many sounds are in "fell"? (three)

Tell me the first sound. (/fff/) Write it.
Repeat with /ĕĕĕ/ and /llll/.
Do Smooth Blending. (/fffĕĕĕllll/) Read the word. (fell)

Repeat with "fly," "my," and "get."

CAUTION

Your children may not need Extra Practice. If in doubt, assess students and include Extra Practice only if needed.

HAVE STUDENTS CHECK AND CORRECT.

❸ DAILY STORY READING

1. First Reading

Have students choral read Fluency Passage 3.

2. Second Reading

- Provide individual turns on sentences. Quietly keep track of errors made by all students in the group.
- After reading, practice any difficult words.

3. Repeated Readings

a. Timed Readings

- Have individual students read the passage while other students track the text with their fingers and whisper read. Time individuals for 30 seconds and encourage each student to work for a personal best.
- For each student, count the number of words read correctly in 30 seconds (words read minus errors). Multiply by two to determine words correct per minute. Record students' scores.

b. Partner Reading—Checkout Opportunity

- Have students partner read. While students are partner reading, listen to individuals read the passage. Work on accuracy or fluency as needed.

Name_____

FLUENCY PASSAGE

What a Frog!	
A frog's habitat is the marsh. The frog	8
is in the weeds where it is cool and wet.	18
The frog eats an insect when it lands	26
nearby. When a fish swims by, the frog	34
eats it. The frog eats, swims, and sings.	42

My goal is to read with 0–2 errors. This is what I did:

Have students read the sentences. Time individual students for 30 seconds; mark errors. To determine words correct per minute (wcpm), count words read in 30 seconds, subtract errors, multiply times two, and record on the chart. If student completes the passage in less than 30 seconds, have him or her return to the top and continue reading. (Repeated readings may be completed with older students, assistants, or parents.)

Reading	1st	2nd	3rd	4th
Errors				
Words/ 30 seconds				
wcpm				

66

① DECODING PRACTICE 4 REVIEW

For each row, mix group and individual turns, independent of your voice.

② WORD DICTATION

Have students count the sounds in each word with their fingers, identify and write each sound, and then read the word. Use the words in sentences as needed.

fast, big, frog, not

The first word is "fast." We're going to count the sounds in "fast."
Tell me the first sound. **Hold up one finger.** (/fff/)

Repeat with /aaa/, /sss/, and /t/.
How many sounds are in "fast"? (Four)

Tell me the first sound. (/fff/) Write it.

Repeat with /aaa/, /sss/, and /t/.
Do Smooth Blending. (/fffaaassst/) Read the word. (fast)

Repeat with "big," "frog," and "not."

CAUTION

Your children may not need Extra Practice. If in doubt, assess students and include Extra Practice only if needed.

HAVE STUDENTS CHECK AND CORRECT.

③ DAILY STORY READING

1. First Reading

Have students choral read Fluency Passage 4.

2. Second Reading

- Provide individual turns on sentences. Quietly keep track of errors made by all students in the group.
- After reading, practice any difficult words.

3. Repeated Readings

a. Timed Readings

- Have individual students read the passage while other students track the text with their fingers and whisper read. Time individuals for 30 seconds and encourage each student to work for a personal best.
- For each student, count the number of words read correctly in 30 seconds (words read minus errors). Multiply by two to determine words correct per minute. Record students' scores.

b. Partner Reading—Checkout Opportunity

- Have students partner read. While students are partner reading, listen to individuals read the passage. Work on accuracy or fluency as needed.

Name_____

FLUENCY PASSAGE

The Foolish Ant	
There was a little ant who wanted	7
to fly. This couldn't work because she had	15
no wings. Still that ant said, "If I go fast,	25
I bet I can fly." So off she ran. Could	35
she fly? No! At last she said, "It's a fact.	45
This little insect cannot fly."	50

My goal is to read with 0–2 errors. This is what I did:

Have students read the sentences. Time individual students for 30 seconds; mark errors. To determine words correct per minute (wcpm), count words read in 30 seconds, subtract errors, multiply times two, and record on the chart. If student completes the passage in less than 30 seconds, have him or her return to the top and continue reading. (Repeated readings may be completed with older students, assistants, or parents.)

Reading	1st	2nd	3rd	4th
Errors				
Words/ 30 seconds				
wcpm				